**CONVENTION BETWEEN
THE GOVERNMENT OF THE UNITED STATES OF AMERICA
AND THE GOVERNMENT OF MALTA
FOR THE AVOIDANCE OF DOUBLE TAXATION AND THE
PREVENTION OF FISCAL EVASION
WITH RESPECT TO TAXES ON INCOME**

The Government of the United States of America and the Government of Malta, desiring to conclude a Convention for the avoidance of double taxation and the prevention of fiscal evasion with respect to taxes on income, have agreed as follows:

## Article 1

## GENERAL SCOPE

1.      This Convention shall apply only to persons who are residents of one or both of the Contracting States, except as otherwise provided in the Convention.

2.      This Convention shall not restrict in any manner any benefit now or hereafter accorded:

      a)      by the laws of either Contracting State; or

      b)      by any other agreement to which the Contracting States are parties.

3.      a)      Notwithstanding the provisions of subparagraph b) of paragraph 2 of this Article:

          i)      for purposes of paragraph 3 of Article XXII (Consultation) of the General Agreement on Trade in Services, the Contracting States agree that any question arising as to the interpretation or application of this Convention and, in particular, whether a taxation measure is within the scope of this Convention, shall be determined exclusively in accordance with the provisions of Article 25 (Mutual Agreement Procedure) of this Convention; and

          ii)      the provisions of Article XVII of the General Agreement on Trade in Services shall not apply to a taxation measure unless the competent authorities agree that the measure is not within the scope of Article 24 (Non-Discrimination) of this Convention.

      b)      For the purposes of this paragraph, a "measure" is a law, regulation, rule, procedure, decision, administrative action, or any similar provision or action.

4.      Except to the extent provided in paragraph 5, this Convention shall not affect the taxation by a Contracting State of its residents (as determined under Article 4 (Resident)) and its citizens. Notwithstanding the other provisions of this Convention, a former citizen or former long-term resident of a Contracting State may, for the period of ten years following the loss of such status, be taxed in accordance with the laws of that Contracting State.

5.      The provisions of paragraph 4 shall not affect:

a)      the benefits conferred by a Contracting State under paragraph 2 of Article 9 (Associated Enterprises), paragraphs 1 b), 2, and 5 of Article 17 (Pensions, Social Security, Annuities, Alimony, and Child Support), and Articles 18 (Pension Funds), 23 (Relief from Double Taxation), 24 (Non-Discrimination), and 25 (Mutual Agreement Procedure); and

b)      the benefits conferred by a Contracting State under Articles 19 (Government Service), 20 (Students and Trainees), and 27 (Members of Diplomatic Missions and Consular Posts), upon individuals who are neither citizens of, nor have been admitted for permanent residence in, that State.

6.      An item of income, profit or gain derived through an entity that is fiscally transparent under the laws of either Contracting State shall be considered to be derived by a resident of a State to the extent that the item is treated for purposes of the taxation law of such Contracting State as the income, profit or gain of a resident.

## Article 2

### TAXES COVERED

1.    This Convention shall apply to taxes on income imposed on behalf of a Contracting State irrespective of the manner in which they are levied.

2.    There shall be regarded as taxes on income all taxes imposed on total income, or on elements of income, including taxes on gains from the alienation of property.

3.    The existing taxes to which this Convention shall apply are:

   a)    in the case of the United States: the Federal income taxes imposed by the Internal Revenue Code (but excluding social security and unemployment taxes), and the Federal excise taxes imposed with respect to private foundations;

   b)    in the case of Malta: the income tax.

4.    This Convention shall apply also to any identical or substantially similar taxes that are imposed after the date of signature of the Convention in addition to, or in place of, the existing taxes. The competent authorities of the Contracting States shall notify each other of any changes that have been made in their respective taxation or other laws that significantly affect their obligations under this Convention.

## Article 3

## GENERAL DEFINITIONS

1.     For the purposes of this Convention, unless the context otherwise requires:

a)     the term "person" includes an individual, an estate, a trust, a partnership, a company, and any other body of persons;

b)     the term "company" means any body corporate or any entity that is treated as a body corporate for tax purposes according to the laws of the state in which it is organized;

c)     the terms "enterprise of a Contracting State" and "enterprise of the other Contracting State" mean respectively an enterprise carried on by a resident of a Contracting State, and an enterprise carried on by a resident of the other Contracting State; the terms also include an enterprise carried on by a resident of a Contracting State through an entity that is treated as fiscally transparent in that Contracting State;

d)     the term "enterprise" applies to the carrying on of any business;

e)     the term "business" includes the performance of professional services and of other activities of an independent character;

f)     the term "international traffic" means any transport by a ship or aircraft, except when such transport is solely between places in a Contracting State;

g)     the term "competent authority" means:

i)     in the United States: the Secretary of the Treasury or his delegate; and

ii)     in Malta: the Minister responsible for finance or his authorized representative;

h)     the term "United States" means the United States of America, and includes the states thereof and the District of Columbia; such term also includes the territorial sea thereof and the sea bed and subsoil of the submarine areas adjacent to that territorial sea, over which the United States exercises sovereign rights in accordance with international law; the term, however, does not include

Puerto Rico, the Virgin Islands, Guam or any other United States possession or territory;

i)      the term "Malta" means the Republic of Malta and, when used in a geographical sense, means the Island of Malta, the Island of Gozo and the other islands of the Maltese archipelago including the territorial sea thereof as well as any area of the sea-bed, its sub-soil and the superjacent water column adjacent to the territorial sea, where the Republic of Malta exercises sovereign rights, jurisdiction or control in accordance with international law and its national law, including its legislation relating to the exploration of the Continental Shelf and exploitation of its natural resources;

j)      the term "national" of a Contracting State means:

    i)      any individual possessing the nationality or citizenship of that State; and

    ii)     any legal person, partnership or association deriving its status as such from the laws in force in that State;

k)      the term "pension fund" means any person established in a Contracting State that is:

    i)      in the case of pension funds established in the United States, generally exempt from income taxation, and in the case of pension funds established in Malta, a licensed fund or scheme subject to tax only on income derived from immovable property situated in Malta; and

    ii)     operated principally either:

        A)      to administer or provide pension or retirement benefits; or

        B)      to earn income for the benefit of one or more persons meeting the requirements of subparagraph i) and clause A) of this subparagraph.

2.      As regards the application of the Convention at any time by a Contracting State any term not defined therein shall, unless the context otherwise requires, or the competent authorities agree to a common meaning pursuant to the provisions of Article 25 (Mutual Agreement Procedure), have the meaning which it has at that time under the law of that State for the purposes of the taxes to which the Convention applies, any

meaning under the applicable tax laws of that State prevailing over a meaning given to the term under other laws of that State.

## Article 4

### RESIDENT

1.      For the purposes of this Convention, the term "resident of a Contracting State" means any person who, under the laws of that State, is liable to tax therein by reason of his domicile, residence, citizenship, place of management, place of incorporation, or any other criterion of a similar nature, and also includes that State and any political subdivision or local authority thereof. This term, however, does not include any person who is liable to tax in that State in respect only of income from sources in that State or of profits attributable to a permanent establishment in that State.

2.      The term "resident of a Contracting State" includes:

    a)      a pension fund established in that State; and

    b)      an organization that is established and maintained in that State exclusively for religious, charitable, scientific, artistic, cultural, or educational purposes,

notwithstanding that all or part of its income or gains may be exempt from tax under the domestic law of that State.

3.      Where, by reason of the provisions of paragraph 1, an individual is a resident of both Contracting States, then his status shall be determined as follows:

    a)      he shall be deemed to be a resident only of the State in which he has a permanent home available to him; if he has a permanent home available to him in both States, he shall be deemed to be a resident only of the State with which his personal and economic relations are closer (center of vital interests);

    b)      if the State in which he has his center of vital interests cannot be determined, or if he does not have a permanent home available to him in either State, he shall be deemed to be a resident only of the State in which he has an habitual abode;

    c)      if he has an habitual abode in both States or in neither of them, he shall be deemed to be a resident only of the State of which he is a national;

    d)      if he is a national of both States or of neither of them, the competent authorities of the Contracting States shall endeavor to settle the question by mutual agreement.

4.      Where by reason of the provisions of paragraph 1 a company is a resident of both Contracting States, then if it is incorporated under the laws of one of the Contracting States or a political subdivision thereof, but not under the laws of the other Contracting State or a political subdivision thereof, such company shall be deemed to be a resident of the first-mentioned Contracting State.  In all other cases involving dual resident companies, the competent authorities of the Contracting States shall endeavor to determine the mode of application of the Convention to such company. If the competent authorities do not reach such an agreement, that company will not be treated as a resident of either Contracting State for purposes of its claiming any benefits provided by the Convention.

5.      Where by reason of the provisions of paragraphs 1 and 2 of this Article a person other than an individual or a company is a resident of both Contracting States, the competent authorities of the Contracting States shall by mutual agreement endeavor to determine the mode of application of this Convention to that person.

## Article 5

### PERMANENT ESTABLISHMENT

1.      For the purposes of this Convention, the term "permanent establishment" means a fixed place of business through which the business of an enterprise is wholly or partly carried on.

2.      The term "permanent establishment" includes especially:

    a)      a place of management;

    b)      a branch;

    c)      an office;

    d)      a factory;

    e)      a workshop; and

    f)      a mine, an oil or gas well, a quarry, or any other place of extraction of natural resources.

3.      A building site or construction or installation project, or an installation or drilling rig or ship used for the exploration of natural resources, constitutes a permanent establishment only if it lasts, or the exploration activity continues for more than twelve months.

4.      Notwithstanding the preceding provisions of this Article, the term "permanent establishment" shall be deemed not to include:

    a)      the use of facilities solely for the purpose of storage, display or delivery of goods or merchandise belonging to the enterprise;

    b)      the maintenance of a stock of goods or merchandise belonging to the enterprise solely for the purpose of storage, display or delivery;

    c)      the maintenance of a stock of goods or merchandise belonging to the enterprise solely for the purpose of processing by another enterprise;

    d)      the maintenance of a fixed place of business solely for the purpose of purchasing goods or merchandise, or of collecting information, for the enterprise;

e)      the maintenance of a fixed place of business solely for the purpose of carrying on, for the enterprise, any other activity of a preparatory or auxiliary character;

f)      the maintenance of a fixed place of business solely for any combination of the activities mentioned in subparagraphs a) through e), provided that the overall activity of the fixed place of business resulting from this combination is of a preparatory or auxiliary character.

5.      Notwithstanding the provisions of paragraphs 1 and 2, where a person -- other than an agent of an independent status to whom paragraph 6 applies -- is acting on behalf of an enterprise and has and habitually exercises in a Contracting State an authority to conclude contracts that are binding on the enterprise, that enterprise shall be deemed to have a permanent establishment in that State in respect of any activities that the person undertakes for the enterprise, unless the activities of such person are limited to those mentioned in paragraph 4 that, if exercised through a fixed place of business, would not make this fixed place of business a permanent establishment under the provisions of that paragraph.

6.      An enterprise shall not be deemed to have a permanent establishment in a Contracting State merely because it carries on business in that State through a broker, general commission agent, or any other agent of an independent status, provided that such persons are acting in the ordinary course of their business as independent agents.

7.      The fact that a company that is a resident of a Contracting State controls or is controlled by a company that is a resident of the other Contracting State, or that carries on business in that other State (whether through a permanent establishment or otherwise), shall not be taken into account in determining whether either company has a permanent establishment in that other State.

## Article 6

## INCOME FROM REAL (IMMOVABLE) PROPERTY

1.      Income derived by a resident of a Contracting State from real (immovable) property, including income from agriculture or forestry, situated in the other Contracting State may be taxed in that other State.

2.      The term "real (immovable) property" shall have the meaning which it has under the law of the Contracting State in which the property in question is situated. The term shall in any case include property accessory to real (immovable) property (including livestock and equipment used in agriculture and forestry), rights to which the provisions of general law respecting landed property apply, usufruct of real (immovable) property and rights to variable or fixed payments as consideration for the working of, or the right to work, mineral deposits, sources and other natural resources. Ships and aircraft shall not be regarded as real (immovable) property.

3.      The provisions of paragraph 1 shall apply to income derived from the direct use, letting, or use in any other form of real (immovable) property.

4.      The provisions of paragraphs 1 and 3 shall also apply to the income from real (immovable) property of an enterprise.

5.      A resident of a Contracting State who is liable to tax in the other Contracting State on income from real (immovable) property situated in the other Contracting State may elect for any taxable year to compute the tax on such income on a net basis as if such income were business profits attributable to a permanent establishment in such other State. In the case of income from real (immovable) property situated in the United States, any such election shall be binding for the taxable year of the election and all subsequent taxable years unless the competent authority of the United States agrees to terminate the election.

## Article 7

### BUSINESS PROFITS

1.      The profits of an enterprise of a Contracting State shall be taxable only in that State unless the enterprise carries on business in the other Contracting State through a permanent establishment situated therein. If the enterprise carries on business as aforesaid, the profits of the enterprise may be taxed in the other State but only so much of them as are attributable to that permanent establishment.

2.      Subject to the provisions of paragraph 3, where an enterprise of a Contracting State carries on business in the other Contracting State through a permanent establishment situated therein, there shall in each Contracting State be attributed to that permanent establishment the profits that it might be expected to make if it were a distinct and independent enterprise engaged in the same or similar activities under the same or similar conditions. For this purpose, the profits to be attributed to the permanent establishment shall include only the profits derived from the assets used, risks assumed and activities performed by the permanent establishment.

3.      In determining the profits of a permanent establishment, there shall be allowed as deductions expenses that are incurred for the purposes of the permanent establishment, including executive and general administrative expenses so incurred, whether in the State in which the permanent establishment is situated or elsewhere.

4.      No profits shall be attributed to a permanent establishment by reason of the mere purchase by that permanent establishment of goods or merchandise for the enterprise.

5.      For the purposes of the preceding paragraphs, the profits to be attributed to the permanent establishment shall be determined by the same method year by year unless there is good and sufficient reason to the contrary.

6.      Where profits include items of income that are dealt with separately in other Articles of the Convention, then the provisions of those Articles shall not be affected by the provisions of this Article.

7.      In applying this Article, paragraph 6 of Article 10 (Dividends), paragraph 5 of Article 11 (Interest), paragraph 4 of Article 12 (Royalties), paragraph 3 of Article 13 (Gains), and paragraph 2 of Article 21 (Other Income), any income or gain attributable to a permanent establishment during its existence is taxable in the Contracting State where such permanent establishment is situated even if the payments are deferred until such permanent establishment has ceased to exist.

## Article 8

### SHIPPING AND AIR TRANSPORT

1.     Profits of an enterprise of a Contracting State from the operation of ships or aircraft in international traffic shall be taxable only in that State.

2.     For purposes of this Article, profits from the operation of ships or aircraft include, but are not limited to:

    a)     profits from the rental of ships or aircraft on a full (time or voyage) basis;

    b)     profits from the rental on a bareboat basis of ships or aircraft if the rental income is incidental to profits from the operation of ships or aircraft in international traffic; and

    c)     profits from the rental on a bareboat basis of ships or aircraft if such ships or aircraft are operated in international traffic by the lessee.

Profits derived by an enterprise from the inland transport of property or passengers within either Contracting State shall be treated as profits from the operation of ships or aircraft in international traffic if such transport is undertaken as part of international traffic.

3.     Profits of an enterprise of a Contracting State from the use, maintenance, or rental of containers (including trailers, barges, and related equipment for the transport of containers) shall be taxable only in that Contracting State, except to the extent that those containers are used for transport solely between places within the other Contracting State.

4.     The provisions of paragraphs 1 and 3 shall also apply to profits from participation in a pool, a joint business, or an international operating agency.

## Article 9

## ASSOCIATED ENTERPRISES

1.    Where:

a)    an enterprise of a Contracting State participates directly or indirectly in the management, control or capital of an enterprise of the other Contracting State; or

b)    the same persons participate directly or indirectly in the management, control, or capital of an enterprise of a Contracting State and an enterprise of the other Contracting State,

and in either case conditions are made or imposed between the two enterprises in their commercial or financial relations that differ from those that would be made between independent enterprises, then any profits that, but for those conditions, would have accrued to one of the enterprises, but by reason of those conditions have not so accrued, may be included in the profits of that enterprise and taxed accordingly.

2.    Where a Contracting State includes in the profits of an enterprise of that State, and taxes accordingly, profits on which an enterprise of the other Contracting State has been charged to tax in that other State, and the other Contracting State agrees that the profits so included are profits that would have accrued to the enterprise of the first-mentioned State if the conditions made between the two enterprises had been those that would have been made between independent enterprises, then that other State shall make an appropriate adjustment to the amount of the tax charged therein on those profits. In determining such adjustment, due regard shall be had to the other provisions of this Convention and the competent authorities of the Contracting States shall if necessary consult each other.

## Article 10

## DIVIDENDS

1.      Dividends paid by a company that is a resident of a Contracting State to a resident of the other Contracting State may be taxed in that other State.

2.      However, such dividends may also be taxed in the Contracting State of which the company paying the dividends is a resident and according to the laws of that State, but:

> a)      if the dividends are paid by a company that is a resident of the United States to a resident of Malta who is the beneficial owner thereof, except as otherwise provided in this Convention, the tax charged by the United States shall not exceed:
>
>> i)      5 percent of the gross amount of the dividends if the beneficial owner is a company that owns directly at least 10 percent of the voting stock of the company paying the dividends;
>>
>> ii)      15 percent of the gross amount of the dividends in all other cases.
>
> b)      if the dividends are paid by a company that is a resident of Malta to a resident of the United States who is the beneficial owner thereof, the tax charged by Malta on the gross amount of the dividends shall not exceed that Malta tax chargeable on the profits out of which the dividends are paid.

This paragraph shall not affect the taxation of the company in respect of the profits out of which the dividends are paid.

3.      Notwithstanding paragraph 2, dividends shall not be taxed in the Contracting State of which the company paying the dividends is a resident if:

> a)      the beneficial owner of the dividends is a pension fund that is a resident of the other Contracting State; and
>
> b)      such dividends are not derived from the carrying on of a trade or business by the pension fund or through an associated enterprise.

4.      a)      Clause i) of subparagraph a) of paragraph 2 shall not apply in the case of dividends paid by a U.S. Regulated Investment Company (RIC) or a U.S. Real Estate Investment Trust (REIT). In the case of dividends paid by a RIC, clause ii) of subparagraph a) of paragraph 2 and paragraph 3 shall apply. In the case of dividends paid by a REIT, clause ii) of subparagraph a) of paragraph 2 and

paragraph 3 shall apply only if:

> i) the beneficial owner of the dividends is an individual or pension fund, in either case holding an interest of not more than 10 percent in the REIT;

> ii) the dividends are paid with respect to a class of stock that is publicly traded and the beneficial owner of the dividends is a person holding an interest of not more than 5 percent of any class of the REIT's stock; or

> iii) the beneficial owner of the dividends is a person holding an interest of not more than 10 percent in the REIT and the REIT is diversified.

b) For purposes of this paragraph, a REIT shall be "diversified" if the value of no single interest in real property exceeds 10 percent of its total interests in real property. For the purposes of this rule, foreclosure property shall not be considered an interest in real property. Where a REIT holds an interest in a partnership, it shall be treated as owning directly a proportion of the partnership's interests in real property corresponding to its interest in the partnership.

5.    For purposes of this Article, the term "dividends" means income from shares or other rights, not being debt-claims, participating in profits, as well as income that is subjected to the same taxation treatment as income from shares under the laws of the State of which the payer is a resident.

6.    The provisions of paragraphs 2 through 4 shall not apply if the beneficial owner of the dividends, being a resident of a Contracting State, carries on business in the other Contracting State, of which the payer is a resident, through a permanent establishment situated therein, and the holding in respect of which the dividends are paid is effectively connected with such permanent establishment. In such case the provisions of Article 7 (Business Profits) shall apply.

7.    A Contracting State may not impose any tax on dividends paid by a resident of the other State, except insofar as the dividends are paid to a resident of the first-mentioned State or the dividends are attributable to a permanent establishment, nor may it impose tax on a corporation's undistributed profits, except as provided in paragraph 8, even if the dividends paid or the undistributed profits consist wholly or partly of profits or income arising in that State.

8.    a) A company that is a resident of one of the States and that has a permanent establishment in the other State or that is subject to tax in the other State on a net basis on its income that may be taxed in the other State under Article 6 (Income

from Real (Immovable) Property) or under paragraph 1 of Article 13 (Gains) may be subject in that other State to a tax in addition to the tax allowable under the other provisions of this Convention.

b)      Such tax, however, may be imposed:

        i)      on only the portion of the business profits of the company attributable to the permanent establishment and the portion of the income referred to in subparagraph a) that is subject to tax under Article 6 or under paragraph 1 of Article 13 that, in the case of the United States, represents the dividend equivalent amount of such profits or income and, in the case of Malta, is an amount that is analogous to the dividend equivalent amount; and

        ii)      at a rate not in excess of the rate specified in clause i) of subparagraph a) of paragraph 2.

## Article 11

## INTEREST

1.    Interest arising in a Contracting State and beneficially owned by a resident of the other Contracting State may be taxed in that other State.

2.    Such interest may also be taxed in the Contracting State in which it arises, and according to the laws of that State, but the tax so charged shall not exceed 10 percent of the gross amount of the interest.

3.    Notwithstanding the provisions of paragraphs 1 and 2:

a)    interest arising in the United States that is contingent interest of a type that does not qualify as portfolio interest under United States law may be taxed by the United States but, if the beneficial owner of the interest is a resident of Malta, the interest may be taxed at a rate not exceeding 15 percent of the gross amount of the interest; and

b)    interest that is an excess inclusion with respect to a residual interest in a real estate mortgage investment conduit may be taxed by each State in accordance with its domestic law.

4.    The term "interest" as used in this Article means income from debt-claims of every kind, whether or not secured by mortgage, and whether or not carrying a right to participate in the debtor's profits, and in particular, income from government securities and income from bonds or debentures, including premiums or prizes attaching to such securities, bonds or debentures, and all other income that is subjected to the same taxation treatment as income from money lent by the taxation law of the Contracting State in which the income arises. Income dealt with in Article 10 (Dividends) and penalty charges for late payment shall not be regarded as interest for the purposes of this Convention.

5.    The provisions of paragraphs 1, 2, and 3 shall not apply if the beneficial owner of the interest, being a resident of a Contracting State, carries on business in the other Contracting State, in which the interest arises, through a permanent establishment situated therein, and the debt-claim in respect of which the interest is paid is effectively connected with such permanent establishment. In such case the provisions of Article 7 (Business Profits) shall apply.

6.    Interest shall be deemed to arise in a Contracting State where the payer is a resident of that State. Where, however, the person paying the interest, whether the person is a resident of a Contracting State or not, has in a Contracting State a permanent

establishment in connection with which the indebtedness on which the interest is paid was incurred, and such interest is borne by such permanent establishment, then such interest shall be deemed to arise in the State in which the permanent establishment is situated.

7.      Where, by reason of a special relationship between the payer and the beneficial owner or between both of them and some other person, the amount of the interest, having regard to the debt-claim for which it is paid, exceeds the amount which would have been agreed upon by the payer and the beneficial owner in the absence of such relationship, the provisions of this Article shall apply only to the last-mentioned amount. In such case the excess part of the payments shall remain taxable according to the laws of each State, due regard being had to the other provisions of this Convention.

8.      In the case of the United States, the excess, if any, of the amount of interest allocable to the profits of a company resident in the other Contracting State that are either attributable to a permanent establishment in the United States or subject to tax in the United States under Article 6 (Income from Real (Immovable) Property) or paragraph 1 of Article 13 (Gains) over the interest paid by that permanent establishment or trade or business in the United States shall be deemed to arise in the United States and be beneficially owned by a resident of the other Contracting State. The tax imposed under this Article on such interest shall not exceed the rate specified in paragraph 2.

## Article 12

## ROYALTIES

1.     Royalties arising in a Contracting State and beneficially owned by a resident of the other Contracting State may be taxed in that other State.

2.     Such royalties may also be taxed in the Contracting State in which they arise, and according to the laws of that State, but the tax so charged shall not exceed 10 percent of the gross amount of the royalties.

3.     For purposes of this Article, the term "royalties" means:

> a)     payments of any kind received as a consideration for the use of, or the right to use, any copyright of literary, artistic, scientific or other work (including cinematographic films), any patent, trademark, design or model, plan, secret formula or process, or for information concerning industrial, commercial or scientific experience; and

> b)     gain derived from the alienation of any property described in subparagraph a), to the extent that such gain is contingent on the productivity, use, or disposition of the property.

4.     The provisions of paragraphs 1 and 2 shall not apply if the beneficial owner of the royalties, being a resident of a Contracting State, carries on business in the other Contracting State through a permanent establishment situated therein and the right or property in respect of which the royalties are paid is effectively connected with such permanent establishment. In such case the provisions of Article 7 (Business Profits) shall apply.

5.     Royalties shall be deemed to arise in a Contracting State when they are in consideration for the use of, or the right to use, property, information or experience in that State.

6.     Where, by reason of a special relationship between the payer and the beneficial owner or between both of them and some other person, the amount of the royalties, having regard to the use, right, or information for which they are paid, exceeds the amount which would have been agreed upon by the payer and the beneficial owner in the absence of such relationship, the provisions of this Article shall apply only to the last-mentioned amount. In such case the excess part of the payments shall remain taxable according to the laws of each Contracting State, due regard being had to the other provisions of the Convention.

## Article 13

## GAINS

1.     Gains derived by a resident of a Contracting State that are attributable to the alienation of real (immovable) property situated in the other Contracting State may be taxed in that other State.

2.     For the purposes of this Article the term "real (immovable) property situated in the other Contracting State" shall include:

   a)     real (immovable) property referred to in Article 6 (Income from Real (Immovable) Property);

   b)     where that other State is the United States, a United States real property interest; and

   c)     where that other State is Malta,

      i)     shares, including rights to acquire shares, in a company resident in Malta whose assets consist wholly or principally of real (immovable) property referred to in subparagraph a) of this paragraph situated in Malta; and

      ii)     an interest in a partnership or trust to the extent that the assets of the partnership or trust consist of real (immovable) property situated in Malta, or of shares referred to in clause i) of this sub-paragraph.

3.     Gains from the alienation of movable property forming part of the business property of a permanent establishment that an enterprise of a Contracting State has in the other Contracting State, including such gains from the alienation of such a permanent establishment (alone or with the whole enterprise), may be taxed in that other State.

4.     Gains derived by an enterprise of a Contracting State from the alienation of ships or aircraft operated or used in international traffic or personal property pertaining to the operation or use of such ships or aircraft shall be taxable only in that State.

5.     Gains derived by an enterprise of a Contracting State from the alienation of containers (including trailers, barges and related equipment for the transport of containers) used for the transport of goods or merchandise shall be taxable only in that State, unless those containers are used for transport solely between places within the

other Contracting State.

6.     Gains from the alienation of any property other than property referred to in paragraphs 1 through 5 and other than gain described in subparagraph b) of paragraph 3 of Article 12 (Royalties) shall be taxable only in the Contracting State of which the alienator is a resident.

## Article 14

### INCOME FROM EMPLOYMENT

1.      Subject to the provisions of Articles 15 (Directors' Fees), 17 (Pensions, Social Security, Annuities, Alimony, and Child Support) and 19 (Government Service), salaries, wages, and other similar remuneration derived by a resident of a Contracting State in respect of an employment shall be taxable only in that State unless the employment is exercised in the other Contracting State. If the employment is so exercised, such remuneration as is derived therefrom may be taxed in that other State.

2.      Notwithstanding the provisions of paragraph 1, remuneration derived by a resident of a Contracting State in respect of an employment exercised in the other Contracting State shall be taxable only in the first-mentioned State if:

> a)      the recipient is present in the other State for a period or periods not exceeding in the aggregate 183 days in any twelve month period commencing or ending in the taxable year concerned;

> b)      the remuneration is paid by, or on behalf of, an employer who is not a resident of the other State; and

> c)      the remuneration is not borne by a permanent establishment which the employer has in the other State.

3.      Notwithstanding the preceding provisions of this Article, remuneration described in paragraph 1 that is derived by a resident of a Contracting State in respect of an employment as a member of the regular complement of a ship or aircraft operated in international traffic shall be taxable only in that State.

## Article 15

## DIRECTORS' FEES

Directors' fees and other compensation derived by a resident of a Contracting State for services rendered in the other Contracting State in his capacity as a member of the board of directors of a company that is a resident of the other Contracting State may be taxed in that other Contracting State.

## Article 16

### ENTERTAINERS AND SPORTSMEN

1.      Income derived by a resident of a Contracting State as an entertainer, such as a theater, motion picture, radio, or television artiste, or a musician, or as a sportsman, from his personal activities as such exercised in the other Contracting State, which income would be exempt from tax in that other Contracting State under the provisions of Articles 7 (Business Profits) and 14 (Income from Employment) may be taxed in that other State, except where the amount of the gross receipts derived by such entertainer or sportsman, including expenses reimbursed to him or borne on his behalf, from such activities does not exceed twenty thousand United States dollars ($20,000) or its equivalent in Euros for the taxable year of the payment.

2.      Where income in respect of activities exercised by an entertainer or a sportsman in his capacity as such accrues not to the entertainer or sportsman himself but to another person, that income, notwithstanding the provisions of Article 7 (Business Profits) or 14 (Income from Employment), may be taxed in the Contracting State in which the activities of the entertainer or sportsman are exercised unless the contract pursuant to which the personal activities are performed allows that other person to designate the individual who is to perform the personal activities.

## Article 17

## PENSIONS, SOCIAL SECURITY, ANNUITIES,
## ALIMONY, AND CHILD SUPPORT

1.    a)    Pensions and other similar remuneration beneficially owned by a resident of a Contracting State shall be taxable only in that State.

b)    Notwithstanding subparagraph a), the amount of any such pension or remuneration arising in a Contracting State that, when received, would be exempt from taxation in that State if the beneficial owner were a resident thereof shall be exempt from taxation in the Contracting State of which the beneficial owner is a resident.

2.    Notwithstanding the provisions of paragraph 1, payments made by a Contracting State under provisions of the social security or similar legislation of that State to a resident of the other Contracting State or to a citizen of the United States shall be taxable only in the first-mentioned State.

3.    Annuities derived and beneficially owned by an individual resident of a Contracting State shall be taxable only in that State. The term "annuities" as used in this paragraph means a stated sum paid periodically at stated times during a specified number of years, or for life, under an obligation to make the payments in return for adequate and full consideration (other than services rendered).

4.    Alimony paid by a resident of a Contracting State to a resident of the other Contracting State shall be taxable only in that other State. The term "alimony" as used in this paragraph means periodic payments made pursuant to a written separation agreement or a decree of divorce, separate maintenance, or compulsory support, which payments are taxable to the recipient under the laws of the State of which he is a resident.

5.    Periodic payments, not dealt with in paragraph 4, for the support of a child made pursuant to a written separation agreement or a decree of divorce, separate maintenance, or compulsory support, paid by a resident of a Contracting State to a resident of the other Contracting State, shall be exempt from tax in both Contracting States.

## Article 18

### PENSION FUNDS

Where an individual who is a resident of one of the States is a member or beneficiary of, or participant in, a pension fund that is a resident of the other State, income earned by the pension fund may be taxed as income of that individual only when, and, subject to the provisions of paragraph 1 of Article 17 (Pensions, Social Security, Annuities, Alimony, and Child Support), to the extent that, it is paid to, or for the benefit of, that individual from the pension fund (and not transferred to another pension fund in that other State).

## Article 19

## GOVERNMENT SERVICE

1.      Notwithstanding the provisions of Articles 14 (Income from Employment), 15 (Directors' Fees), 16 (Entertainers and Sportsmen) and 20 (Students and Trainees):

a)      Salaries, wages and other remuneration, other than a pension, paid to an individual in respect of services rendered to a Contracting State or a political subdivision or local authority thereof shall, subject to the provisions of subparagraph b), be taxable only in that State;

b)      such remuneration, however, shall be taxable only in the other Contracting State if the services are rendered in that State and the individual is a resident of that State who:

i)      is a national of that State; or

ii)      did not become a resident of that State solely for the purpose of rendering the services.

2.      Notwithstanding the provisions of paragraph 1 of Article 17 (Pensions, Social Security, Annuities, Alimony, and Child Support):

a)      any pension and other similar remuneration paid by, or out of funds created by, a Contracting State or a political subdivision or a local authority thereof to an individual in respect of services rendered to that State or subdivision or authority (other than a payment to which paragraph 2 of Article 17 applies) shall, subject to the provisions of subparagraph b), be taxable only in that State;

b)      such pension, however, shall be taxable only in the other Contracting State if the individual is a resident of, and a national of, that State.

3.      The provisions of Articles 14 (Income from Employment), 15 (Directors' Fees), 16 (Entertainers and Sportsmen) and 17 (Pensions, Social Security, Annuities, Alimony, and Child Support) shall apply to salaries, wages and other remuneration, and to pensions, in respect of services rendered in connection with a business carried on by a Contracting State or a political subdivision or a local authority thereof.

## Article 20

### STUDENTS AND TRAINEES

1.     Payments, other than compensation for personal services, received by a student or business trainee who is, or was immediately before visiting a Contracting State, a resident of the other Contracting State, and who is present in the first-mentioned State for the purpose of his full-time education or for his full-time training, shall not be taxed in that State, provided that such payments arise outside that State, and are for the purpose of his maintenance, education or training. The exemption from tax provided by this paragraph shall apply to a business trainee only for a period of time not exceeding one year from the date the business trainee first arrives in the first-mentioned Contracting State for the purpose of training.

2.     A student or business trainee within the meaning of paragraph 1 shall be exempt from tax by the Contracting State in which the individual is temporarily present with respect to income from personal services in an aggregate amount equal to $9,000 or its equivalent in Euros annually. The competent authorities shall, every five years, adjust the amount provided in this subparagraph to the extent necessary to take into account changes in the U.S. personal exemption and the standard deduction and in the Maltese personal tax rates.

3.     For purposes of this Article, a business trainee is an individual:

   a)     who is temporarily in a Contracting State for the purpose of securing training required to qualify the individual to practice a profession or professional specialty; or

   b)     who is temporarily in a Contracting State as an employee of, or under contract with, a resident of the other Contracting State, for the primary purpose of acquiring technical, professional, or business experience from a person other than that resident of the other Contracting State (or a person related to such resident of the other Contracting State).

## Article 21

## OTHER INCOME

1. Items of income beneficially owned by a resident of a Contracting State, wherever arising, not dealt with in the foregoing Articles of this Convention shall be taxable in that State.

2. The provisions of paragraph 1 shall not apply to income, other than income from real (immovable) property as defined in paragraph 2 of Article 6 (Income from Real (Immovable) Property), if the beneficial owner of the income, being a resident of a Contracting State, carries on business in the other Contracting State through a permanent establishment situated therein and the income is attributable to such permanent establishment. In such case the provisions of Article 7 (Business Profits) shall apply.

3. Notwithstanding the provisions of paragraphs 1 and 2, items of income of a resident of one of the Contracting States not dealt with in the foregoing Articles of this Convention from sources in the other Contracting State may also be taxed in the other Contracting State, but the tax so charged shall not exceed 10 percent of the amount of such items.

## Article 22

## LIMITATION ON BENEFITS

1.     Except as otherwise provided in this Article, a resident of one of the Contracting States that derives income from the other Contracting State shall be entitled, in that other Contracting State, to all the benefits of this Convention otherwise accorded to residents of a Contracting State only if such resident is a "qualified person" as defined in paragraph 2 of this Article and satisfies any other conditions specified in the Convention for the obtaining of such benefits.

2.     A resident of one of the Contracting States is a qualified person for a taxable year only if such resident is either:

a)     an individual;

b)     a Contracting State, political subdivision or local authority thereof;

c)     a company, if:

i)

A)     its principal class of shares (and any disproportionate class of shares) is listed on a recognized stock exchange located in the Contracting State of which the company is a resident;

B)     its principal class of shares (and any disproportionate class of shares) is regularly traded on one or more recognized stock exchanges located in the Contracting State of which the company is a resident;

C)     its principal class of shares is primarily traded on one or more recognized stock exchanges located in the Contracting State of which the company is a resident; and

D)     the company satisfies the requirements of clause ii) of subparagraph f) of this paragraph; or

ii)

A)     at least 75 percent of each such class of shares in the company is owned directly or indirectly by companies entitled to benefits under clause i), provided that in the case of indirect ownership, each intermediate owner is a resident of the same

Contracting State entitled to benefits of the Convention under this clause ii); and

B)  the company satisfies the requirements of clause ii) of subparagraph f) of this paragraph;

d)  an entity described in subparagraph b) of paragraph 2 of Article 4 (Resident) that is generally exempt from income taxation in its Contracting State of residence;

e)  a pension fund, provided that more than 75 percent of the beneficiaries, members or participants of the pension fund are individuals who are residents of either Contracting State; or

f)  a person other than an individual, if:

i)  on at least half the days of the taxable year at least 75 percent of each class of shares or other beneficial interests in the person is owned, directly or indirectly, by residents of that Contracting State that are entitled to the benefits of this Convention under subparagraph a), subparagraph b), clause i) of subparagraph c), subparagraph d), or subparagraph e) of this paragraph, provided that, in the case of indirect ownership, each intermediate owner is a qualified person that is a resident of that Contracting State; and

ii)  less than 25 percent of the person's gross income for the taxable year, as determined in the person's State of residence, is paid or accrued, directly or indirectly, to persons who are not residents of either Contracting State entitled to the benefits of this Convention under subparagraph a), subparagraph b), clause i) of subparagraph c), subparagraph d), or subparagraph e) of this paragraph (other than in the form of arm's length payments in the ordinary course of business for services or tangible property).

3.  Notwithstanding that a company that is a resident of a Contracting State may not be a qualified person, it shall be entitled to all the benefits of this Convention otherwise accorded to residents of a Contracting State with respect to an item of income if it satisfies any other specified conditions for the obtaining of such benefits and:

a)  at least 95 percent of each class of shares of the company are owned, directly or indirectly, by seven or fewer persons who are equivalent beneficiaries; and

b)      less than 25 percent of the company's gross income for the taxable year in which the item of income arises is paid or accrued, directly or indirectly, to persons who are not equivalent beneficiaries (other than in the form of arm's length payments in the ordinary course of business for services or tangible property).

4.

a)      A resident of a Contracting State will be entitled to benefits of the Convention with respect to an item of income derived from the other State, regardless of whether the resident is a qualified person, if:

i)      the resident is engaged in the active conduct of a trade or business in the first-mentioned State (other than the business of making or managing investments for the resident's own account, unless these activities are banking or insurance activities carried on by a bank or insurance company), and the income derived from the other Contracting State is derived in connection with, or is incidental to, that trade or business; and

ii)      the resident satisfies the requirements of clause ii) of subparagraph f) of paragraph 2.

b)      If a resident of a Contracting State derives an item of income from a trade or business activity conducted by that resident in the other Contracting State, or derives an item of income arising in the other Contracting State from a related person, the conditions described in clause i) of subparagraph a) shall be considered to be satisfied with respect to such item only if the trade or business activity carried on by the resident in the first-mentioned Contracting State is substantial in relation to the trade or business activity carried on by the resident or such person in the other Contracting State. A trade or business will be deemed substantial if, for each of the three preceding taxable years, the asset value, the gross income, and the payroll expense that are related to the trade or business in the first-mentioned Contracting State each equals at least 10 percent of the resident's (and any related parties') proportionate share of the asset value, gross income and payroll expense, respectively, related to the activity that generated the income in the other Contracting State, and the average of the three ratios in each such year exceeds 15 percent.

c)      For purposes of applying this paragraph, activities conducted by persons connected to a person shall be deemed to be conducted by such person. A person shall be connected to another if one possesses at least 50 percent of the beneficial interest in the other (or, in the case of a company, at least 50 percent of the aggregate vote and value of the company's shares or of the beneficial equity interest in the company) or another person possesses at least 50 percent of the beneficial interest (or, in the case of a company, at least 50 percent of the aggregate vote and value of the company's shares or of the beneficial equity interest in the company) in each person. In any case, a person shall be considered to be connected to another if, based on all the relevant facts and circumstances, one has control of the other or both are under the control of the same person or persons.

5.      Notwithstanding the preceding provisions of this Article, where an enterprise of a Contracting State derives income from the other Contracting State, and that income is attributable to a permanent establishment which that enterprise has in a third jurisdiction, the tax benefits that would otherwise apply under the other provisions of the Convention will not apply to that income if the combined tax that is actually paid with respect to such income in the first-mentioned Contracting State and in the third jurisdiction is less than 60 percent of the tax that would have been payable in the first-mentioned State if the income were earned in that Contracting State by the enterprise and were not attributable to the permanent establishment in the third jurisdiction. Any dividends, interest or royalties to which the provisions of this paragraph apply shall be subject to tax at a rate that shall not exceed 15 percent of the gross amount thereof. Any other income to which the provisions of this paragraph apply will be subject to tax under the provisions of the domestic law of the other Contracting State, notwithstanding any other provision of the Convention.

6.      A person that is a resident of one of the Contracting States, who is not entitled to some or all of the benefits of this Convention because of the foregoing paragraphs, may, nevertheless, be granted benefits of this Convention if the competent authority of the Contracting State in which the income in question arises so determines.

7.      Where under any provision of this Convention income or gains arising in one of the Contracting States are relieved from tax in that Contracting State and, under the law in force in the other Contracting State, a person, in respect of the said income or gains, is subject to tax by reference to the amount thereof which is remitted to or received in that other Contracting State and not by reference to the full amount thereof, then the relief to be allowed under this Convention in the first-mentioned Contracting State shall apply only to so much of the income or gains as is taxed in the other Contracting State.

8.      For the purposes of this Article:

    a)      the term "recognized stock exchange" means:

i)      the NASDAQ System and any stock exchange registered with the U.S. Securities and Exchange Commission as a national securities exchange under the U.S. Securities Exchange Act of 1934;

ii)     the Malta Stock Exchange; and

iii)    any other stock exchange agreed upon by the competent authorities of the Contracting States;

b)      the term "principal class of shares" means the ordinary or common shares of the company, provided that such class of shares represents the majority of the voting power and value of the company. If no single class of ordinary or common shares represents the majority of the aggregate voting power and value of the company, the "principal class of shares" are those classes that in the aggregate represent a majority of the aggregate voting power and value of the company;

c)      the term "disproportionate class of shares" means any class of shares of a company resident in one of the Contracting States that entitles the shareholder to disproportionately higher participation, through dividends, redemption payments or otherwise, in the earnings generated in the other State by particular assets or activities of the company;

d)      For purposes of this paragraph an equivalent beneficiary is a resident of a member state of the European Union or of a European Economic Area state or of Australia or of a party to the North American Free Trade Agreement but only if that resident:

i)

A)      would be entitled to all the benefits of a comprehensive convention for the avoidance of double taxation between any member state of the European Union or a European Economic Area state or any party to the North American Free Trade Agreement or Australia and the State from which the benefits of this Convention are claimed under provisions analogous to subparagraph a), subparagraph b), clause i) of subparagraph c), subparagraph d), or subparagraph e) of paragraph 2 of this Article, provided that if such convention does not contain a comprehensive limitation on benefits article, the person would be a qualified person under subparagraph a), subparagraph b), clause i) of subparagraph c), subparagraph d), or subparagraph e) of paragraph 2 of this Article if such person were a resident of one of the States under Article 4 (Resident) of this Convention; and

B) with respect to income referred to in Articles 10 (Dividends), 11 (Interest) or 12 (Royalties) of this Convention, would be entitled under such convention to a rate of tax with respect to the particular class of income for which benefits are being claimed under this Convention that is at least as low as the rate applicable under this Convention; or

ii) is a resident of a Contracting State that is a qualified person by reason of subparagraph a), subparagraph b), clause i) of subparagraph c), subparagraph d), or subparagraph e) of paragraph 2 of this Article;

e) With respect to dividends, interest or royalties arising in Malta and beneficially owned by a company that is a resident of the United States, a company that is a resident of a member state of the European Union will be treated as satisfying the requirements of clause i) B) of subparagraph d) for purposes of determining whether such United States resident is entitled to benefits under this paragraph if a payment of dividends, interest or royalties arising in Malta and paid directly to such resident of a member state of the European Union would have been exempt from tax pursuant to any directive of the European Union, notwithstanding that the income tax convention between Malta and that other member state of the European Union would provide for a higher rate of tax with respect to such payment than the rate of tax applicable to such United States company under Article 10 (Dividends), 11 (Interest), or 12 (Royalties) of this Convention.

## Article 23

### RELIEF FROM DOUBLE TAXATION

1. In accordance with the provisions and subject to the limitations of the law of the United States (as it may be amended from time to time without changing the general principle hereof), the United States shall allow to a resident or citizen of the United States as a credit against the United States tax on income applicable to residents and citizens:

    a) the income tax paid or accrued to Malta by or on behalf of such resident or citizen; and

    b) in the case of a United States company owning at least 10 percent of the voting stock of a company that is a resident of Malta and from which the United States company receives dividends, the income tax paid or accrued to Malta by or on behalf of the payer with respect to the profits out of which the dividends are paid.

For the purposes of this paragraph, the taxes referred to in paragraphs 3 a) and 4 of Article 2 (Taxes Covered) shall be considered income taxes.

2. In accordance with and subject to the provisions of the law of Malta regarding the allowance of a credit against Malta tax in respect of foreign tax:

    a) where, in accordance with the provisions of this Convention, there is included in a Malta assessment income from sources within the United States, the United States tax on such income shall be allowed as a credit against the relative Malta tax payable thereon; and

    b) where a Maltese company owns at least 10 percent of the voting stock of a company that is a resident of the United States and from which the Maltese company receives dividends that are included in a Malta assessment in accordance with the provisions of this Convention, the income tax paid or accrued to the United States by or on behalf of the payer with respect to the profits out of which the dividends are paid shall, if those profits are included in a Malta assessment, be allowed as a credit against the relative Malta tax payable thereon.

3. For the purposes of applying paragraph 1 of this Article, an item of gross income, as determined under the laws of the United States, derived by a resident of the United States that, under this Convention, may be taxed in Malta shall be deemed to be income

from sources in Malta.

4.      Where a United States citizen is a resident of Malta:

a)      with respect to items of income that under the provisions of this Convention are exempt from United States tax or that are subject to a reduced rate of United States tax when derived by a resident of Malta who is not a United States citizen, Malta shall allow as a credit against Malta tax, only the tax paid, if any, that the United States may impose under the provisions of this Convention, other than taxes that may be imposed solely by reason of citizenship under the saving clause of paragraph 4 of Article 1 (General Scope);

b)      for purposes of applying paragraph 1 to compute United States tax on those items of income referred to in subparagraph a), the United States shall allow as a credit against United States tax the income tax paid to Malta after the credit referred to in subparagraph a); the credit so allowed shall not reduce the portion of the United States tax that is creditable against the Malta tax in accordance with subparagraph a); and

c)      for the exclusive purpose of relieving double taxation in the United States under subparagraph b), items of income referred to in subparagraph a) shall be deemed to arise in Malta to the extent necessary to avoid double taxation of such income under subparagraph b).

## Article 24

### NON-DISCRIMINATION

1.    Nationals of a Contracting State shall not be subjected in the other Contracting State to any taxation or any requirement connected therewith that is more burdensome than the taxation and connected requirements to which nationals of that other State in the same circumstances, in particular with respect to residence, are or may be subjected. This provision shall also apply to persons who are not residents of one or both of the Contracting States.  However, for the purposes of United States taxation, United States nationals who are subject to tax on a worldwide basis are not in the same circumstances as nationals of Malta who are not residents of the United States.

2.    The taxation on a permanent establishment that an enterprise of a Contracting State has in the other Contracting State shall not be less favorably levied in that other State than the taxation levied on enterprises of that other State carrying on the same activities.

3.    The provisions of paragraphs 1 and 2 shall not be construed as obliging a Contracting State to grant to residents of the other Contracting State any personal allowances, reliefs, and reductions for taxation purposes on account of civil status or family responsibilities that it grants to its own residents.

4.    Except where the provisions of paragraph 1 of Article 9 (Associated Enterprises), paragraph 7 of Article 11 (Interest), or paragraph 6 of Article 12 (Royalties) apply, interest, royalties, and other disbursements paid by a resident of a Contracting State to a resident of the other Contracting State shall, for the purpose of determining the taxable profits of the first-mentioned resident, be deductible under the same conditions as if they had been paid to a resident of the first-mentioned State.  Similarly, any debts of a resident of a Contracting State to a resident of the other Contracting State shall, for the purpose of determining the taxable capital of the first-mentioned resident, be deductible under the same conditions as if they had been contracted to a resident of the first-mentioned State.

5.    Enterprises of a Contracting State, the capital of which is wholly or partly owned or controlled, directly or indirectly, by one or more residents of the other Contracting State, shall not be subjected in the first-mentioned State to any taxation or any requirement connected therewith that is more burdensome than the taxation and connected requirements to which other similar enterprises of the first-mentioned State are or may be subjected.

6.      Nothing in this Article shall be construed as preventing either Contracting State from imposing a tax as described in paragraph 8 of Article 10 (Dividends).

7.      The provisions of this Article shall, notwithstanding the provisions of Article 2 (Taxes Covered), apply to taxes of every kind and description imposed by a Contracting State or a political subdivision or local authority thereof.

## Article 25

## MUTUAL AGREEMENT PROCEDURE

1.      Where a person considers that the actions of one or both of the Contracting States result or will result for such person in taxation not in accordance with the provisions of this Convention, it may, irrespective of the remedies provided by the domestic law of those States, and the time limits prescribed in such laws for presenting claims for refund, present its case to the competent authority of either Contracting State.

2.      The competent authority shall endeavor, if the objection appears to it to be justified and if it is not itself able to arrive at a satisfactory solution, to resolve the case by mutual agreement with the competent authority of the other Contracting State, with a view to the avoidance of taxation which is not in accordance with the Convention. Any agreement reached shall be implemented notwithstanding any time limits or other procedural limitations in the domestic law of the Contracting States. Assessment and collection procedures shall be suspended during the period that any mutual agreement proceeding is pending.

3.      The competent authorities of the Contracting States shall endeavor to resolve by mutual agreement any difficulties or doubts arising as to the interpretation or application of the Convention. They also may consult together for the elimination of double taxation in cases not provided for in the Convention. In particular the competent authorities of the Contracting States may agree:

    a)      to the same attribution of income, deductions, credits, or allowances of an enterprise of a Contracting State to its permanent establishment situated in the other Contracting State;

    b)      to the same allocation of income, deductions, credits, or allowances between persons;

    c)      to the settlement of conflicting application of the Convention, including conflicts regarding:

        i)      the characterization of particular items of income;

        ii)     the characterization of persons;

        iii)    the application of source rules with respect to particular items of

        income;

      iv)     the meaning of any term used in the Convention;

      v)     the timing of particular items of income;

d)     to advance pricing arrangements; and

e)     to the application of the provisions of domestic law regarding penalties, fines, and interest in a manner consistent with the purposes of the Convention.

4.     The competent authorities also may agree to increases in any specific dollar amounts referred to in the Convention to reflect economic or monetary developments.

5.     The competent authorities of the Contracting States may communicate with each other directly, including through a joint commission, for the purpose of reaching an agreement in the sense of the preceding paragraphs.

**Article 26**

**EXCHANGE OF INFORMATION AND ADMINISTRATIVE ASSISTANCE**

1.     The competent authorities of the Contracting States shall exchange such information as may be relevant for carrying out the provisions of this Convention or of the domestic laws of the Contracting States concerning taxes of every kind imposed by a Contracting State to the extent that the taxation thereunder is not contrary to the Convention, including information relating to the assessment or collection of, the enforcement or prosecution in respect of, or the determination of appeals in relation to, such taxes. The exchange of information is not restricted by paragraph 1 of Article 1 (General Scope) or Article 2 (Taxes Covered).

2.     Any information received under this Article by a Contracting State shall be treated as secret in the same manner as information obtained under the domestic laws of that State and shall be disclosed only to persons or authorities (including courts and administrative bodies) involved in the assessment, collection, or administration of, the enforcement or prosecution in respect of, or the determination of appeals in relation to, the taxes referred to above, or the oversight of such functions. Such persons or authorities shall use the information only for such purposes. They may disclose the information in public court proceedings or in judicial decisions. The competent authority of the Contracting State that receives information under the provisions of this Article may, with the written consent of the Contracting State that provided the information, also make available that information to be used for other purposes allowed under the provisions of an existing mutual legal assistance treaty between the Contracting States that allows for the exchange of tax information.

3.     In no case shall the provisions of the preceding paragraphs be construed so as to impose on a Contracting State the obligation:

   a)     to carry out administrative measures at variance with the laws and administrative practice of that or of the other Contracting State;

   b)     to supply information that is not obtainable under the laws or in the normal course of the administration of that or of the other Contracting State;

   c)     to supply information that would disclose any trade, business, industrial, commercial, or professional secret or trade process, or information the disclosure of which would be contrary to public policy (ordre public).

4.     If information is requested by a Contracting State in accordance with this Article, the other Contracting State shall use its information gathering measures to obtain the

requested information, even though that other State may not need such information for its own purposes. The obligation contained in the preceding sentence is subject to the limitations of paragraph 3 but in no case shall such limitation be construed to permit a Contracting State to decline to supply information because it has no domestic interest in such information.

5.      In no case shall the provisions of paragraph 3 be construed to permit a Contracting State to decline to supply information requested by the other Contracting State because the information is held by a bank, other financial institution, nominee or person acting in an agency or a fiduciary capacity or because it relates to ownership interests in a person.

6.      If specifically requested by the competent authority of a Contracting State, the competent authority of the other Contracting State shall provide information under this Article in the form of depositions of witnesses and authenticated copies of unedited original documents (including books, papers, statements, records, accounts, and writings).

7.      The requested State shall allow representatives of the requesting State to enter the requested State to interview individuals and examine books and records with the consent of the persons subject to examination.

8.      The competent authorities of the Contracting States may develop an agreement upon the mode of application of this Article, including agreement to ensure comparable levels of assistance to each of the Contracting States, but in no case will the lack of such agreement relieve a Contracting State of its obligations under this Article.

## Article 27

### MEMBERS OF DIPLOMATIC MISSIONS AND CONSULAR POSTS

Nothing in this Convention shall affect the fiscal privileges of members of diplomatic missions or consular posts under the general rules of international law or under the provisions of special agreements.

## Article 28

### ENTRY INTO FORCE

1.      This Convention shall be subject to ratification in accordance with the applicable procedures of each Contracting State, and instruments of ratification will be exchanged as soon thereafter as possible.

2.      This Convention shall enter into force on the date of the exchange of instruments of ratification, and its provisions shall have effect:

a)      in respect of taxes withheld at source, for amounts paid or credited on or after the first day of the second month next following the date on which the Convention enters into force;

b)      in respect of other taxes, for taxable periods beginning on or after the first day of January next following the date on which the Convention enters into force.

3.      Notwithstanding paragraph 2, the provisions of Article 26 (Exchange of Information and Administrative Assistance) shall have effect from the date of entry into force of this Convention, without regard to the taxable period to which the matter relates.

## Article 29

### TERMINATION

This Convention shall remain in force until terminated by a Contracting State. Either Contracting State may terminate the Convention by giving notice of termination to the other Contracting State through diplomatic channels. In such event, the Convention shall cease to have effect:

    1)    in respect of taxes withheld at source, for amounts paid or credited after the expiration of the 6 month period beginning on the date on which notice of termination was given; and

    2)    in respect of other taxes, for taxable periods beginning on or after the expiration of the 6 month period beginning on the date on which notice of termination was given.

    IN WITNESS WHEREOF, the undersigned, being duly authorized thereto by their respective Governments, have signed this Convention.

    DONE at Valletta, in duplicate, this 8th day of August, 2008.

FOR THE GOVERNMENT OF          FOR THE GOVERNMENT OF
THE UNITED STATES OF AMERICA:    MALTA:


MOLLY BORDONARO          TONIO FENECH

www.ingramcontent.com/pod-product-compliance
Lightning Source LLC
Chambersburg PA
CBHW060649290526
45793CB00001B/466